A WILDLIFE WATCHER'S FIRST GUIDE

Faces in the Forest

RON HIRSCHI

Photographs by

THOMAS D. MANGELSEN

COBBLEHILL BOOKS/Dutton

New York

For Edna and her baby eagles — R.H.

For Mary Rommelfanger — T.M.

Text copyright © 1997 by Ron Hirschi
Photographs copyright © 1997 by Thomas D. Mangelsen
Library of Congress Cataloging-in-Publication Data
Hirschi, Ron
Faces in the forest/Ron Hirschi;
photographs by Thomas D. Mangelsen
p.   cm.—(A Wildlife watcher's first guide)
Summary: Introduces the various animals that live in the forests
of the United States, including beavers, chipmunks, spotted
owls, bears, deer, bobcats, eagles, and others.
ISBN 0-525-65224-8
1. Forest animals—Juvenile literature.   [1. Forest
animals.]   I. Mangelsen, Thomas D., ill.   II. Title.
III. Series: Hirschi, Ron.   Wildlife watcher's first guide.
QL112.H565 1997 591.52′642—dc20 95-48420 CIP AC
Published in the United States by Cobblehill Books,
an affiliate of Dutton Children's Books,
a division of Penguin Books USA Inc.,
375 Hudson Street, New York, New York 10014
Designed by Kathleen Westray
Printed in Hong Kong
First Edition   10 9 8 7 6 5 4 3 2 1

Cassin's finch

Franklin ground squirrel

Elk

DEAR WILDLIFE WATCHER,

Today I went for a hike in the woods with my dog. We saw a rabbit, two deer, and a shiny black raven that was flying overhead. I know more animals live here — I can hear some tiny birds singing high in the treetops and squirrels chattering in the branches. So, we will return another day.

Do you wonder what animals live in your forest? What animal faces can you see in the woods from winter to spring? Can you find tracks of deer, raccoons, and red fox? If you spend the time, could you ever see all our friends in the forest?

YOUR FRIEND,

Ron Hirschi

Can you find all the animals
in your forest? Look closely.
Listen, too. Birds will sing
from up high, squirrels will
hop from branch to branch,
and bears will hide from view.

Red squirrel

But lots of other animal faces are waiting just for you.

Marten

Black-capped chickadee

You can see chickadees calling from the tips of tree branches in almost any woods. They sing winter to spring. Up close, they look like they have little black caps on their heads. Sometimes they hang upside down. Sometimes they will sit in your hand if you offer sunflower seeds.

Red-breasted nuthatch

Nuthatches live with chickadees but act differently. They like to hop up and down tree trunks, searching for bugs. Their slender bills are curved, just right for picking beetles from bark.

White-breasted nuthatch

Crossbills live coast to coast in northern forests and throughout the West. They are a little smaller than robins and have most unusual bills. Like pairs of snippers, their crossed bills help them open pinecones and eat the seeds. Crossbills need clean, cold water for summertime sips.

Red crossbill

Woodpeckers need forests. They help them too, by eating insects harmful to trees. Listen as they hammer tree trunks in search of food or as they build homes. Hairy woodpeckers, downy woodpeckers, and flickers live in many kinds of forest. The much larger pileated woodpecker can only find a home if trees are big and old.

Hairy woodpecker

Pileated woodpeckers make loud, chopping sounds. Smaller woodpeckers, like the downy, are quieter when they chip holes in trees. Nesting holes made by pileated woodpeckers are just right for squirrels, wood ducks, and small owls. Bluebirds, chickadees, or swallows might move into holes made by hairy woodpeckers after they move on to new nesting trees.

Northern flicker

Wood duck

When forests grow along rivers, ponds, and lakes you will find more animals than in any other kind of woods. Where water meets the trees, some surprising forest faces might even appear. Watch the forested shores for ducks that nest in trees.

Common goldeneye

Wood ducks are just one kind of water bird that nests in holes in trees. They like to eat the seeds from oaks and other trees. Goldeneyes, buffleheads, and mergansers also find homes in tree nests.

Sockeye salmon

Fish live in forests too! Some, like salmon and trout, must have trees to survive in their cold and clear woodland streams. The fish eat insects that eat leaves that grow on trees shading their homes.

Great blue herons are one of many predators that might snatch some of the salmon, trout, or other fish. The heron's long bill helps it catch fish. It also helps the long-legged heron stack sticks in its treetop nest. Sometimes more than 100 pairs of herons nest together in colonies up in the tallest of trees. You will know these nesting places if you hear loud, squawking sounds and see the lanky, blue-gray birds fly from water to woods.

Great blue heron

One of the best places to watch wildlife in any woods is where trees are falling down. But how can falling trees be a good thing for animals who need forests?

Where a beaver is doing the cutting, many of the trees are used in the beaver's dam. As the dam creates a pond for the beaver, many other animals also find a home. Deer can drink, fish can swim, and ducks find safe resting places. And, the trees surrounding a beaver's home grow tall and healthy as water from the pond slowly soaks into the forest soil.

Beaver

Beaver lodge

Spotted owl with mouse

A beaver pond also attracts hawks and owls that come to hunt ducks and other birds living in woods at the water's edge.

Sharp-shinned hawk

Great blue heron

Like the heron, a red-tailed hawk builds a stick nest. But it likes to place its treetop nest in forest clearings, or even in a single tree surrounded by meadows and ponds. Watch for its red tail and wide wings as the hawk soars over fields in search of mice, snakes and squirrels.

Red-tailed hawk

Down on the ground, you will find some faces you know and also the tracks of these forest friends. Raccoons leave their hand-shaped prints in soft mud as they search for frogs, mice, and insects.

Raccoon

Chipmunks are friendly faces that might be watching you in almost any forest. They like to hide in tangles of berry bushes, wild roses, and old fallen logs — places just right for beetles, toads, and salamanders too.

Least chipmunk

Black bear

No forest face is more familiar than that of the bear. Black bears live in woods in all corners of our country. They are our smallest bears, but ones to watch from safe distances. They can survive in woods not far from cities, houses, and schools. But they need quiet places to raise their cubs.

Grizzly bears live in forests much wilder, wider, and way out west. They wander mountain meadows and forests, hunting elk, deer, and moose. Grizzlies also eat lots of berries, grass, and pine seeds. This biggest of bears even munches tiny moths for many of its meals.

Grizzly bears

Just like the grizzly, flying forest hunters need lots of space to survive. Spotted owls only live where the oldest forests and tallest trees offer cool shade and special nesting places. The nests might be in a tree that is dying, but still needed. A hollow spot in its ancient trunk might be where the babies are hatched.

The old woods are covered with moss. Ferns grow deep green and the rare spotted owl hunts here — searching for bats, flying squirrels, and even other owls. The baby spotted owl will fly away from its place of birth. But it must find another ancient forest when it is ready to build a nest of its own.

Spotted owls may survive where the beaver cuts some of the trees. They may live near the sounds of a woodpecker, chipping at bark for beetles. But they will not live where too many trees are felled by people who do not value the vanishing ancient forests of the West.

Search for the owls and watch for the other faces in the forest. And let them all show you their own special homes.

Baby spotted owl

Elk

Mule deer

Marten

Searching for More Faces

Once you see one animal, there will be more nearby. Animals live together or near one another for many reasons — some as relatives, some as predators and prey, others because a shared food grows in one place.

Berries, seeds, and water all attract small animals that may, in turn, attract larger animals. A forest can be a kind of community much like our own. Get to know one of these communities and you will likely see the following groups of animals in these places:

Look for chickadees, squirrels, white-tailed deer, chipmunks, toads, and red-tailed hawks in most eastern United States forests such as within Great Smoky Mountains National Park.

Watch eagles, black bear, elk, black-tail deer, chipmunks, Cassin's finches, and chickadees in the Pacific Northwest at Olympic National Park. Spotted owls and salmon can also be seen here.

Rocky Mountain forests are home to mule deer, cougar,

Lazuli bunting

bobcats, grizzly bears, black bears, martens, ravens, lazuli buntings, pine grosbeaks, and flickers.

Pileated woodpeckers, squirrels, downy woodpeckers, white-tailed deer, crossbills, evening grosbeaks, wood ducks, and great blue herons can be seen in coastal forests and woodlands near the Great Lakes.

Texas is a good place to visit to watch for bluebirds, white-tailed deer, raccoons, warblers, robins, and some unusual forest wildlife, including wild pigs.

Salmon, river otters, mink, raccoons, bobcats, trout, and bald eagles can be seen in forests that line rivers from San Francisco north to Alaska.

Watch for herons, otters, beaver, wood ducks, warblers, hummingbirds, and owls throughout the southeastern United States.

Even within the most crowded city, trees will be home to squirrels, warblers, robins, chickadees, red-tailed hawks, and many kinds of woodpeckers, including the pileated.

Evening grosbeak

Bald eagle

Black-capped chickadee

Wood ducks

Beaver

Forest Facts

Chickadees nest in holes, but cannot chisel in wood with their tiny beaks. They need woodpeckers to build homes for them.

Nuthatches eat thousands of insects each year, beetles and others that might otherwise harm trees.

Crossbills cannot survive without the seeds of spruce, pine, hemlock, larch, and fir trees that grow in and form our evergreen forests.

Woodpeckers are the carpenters of the treetops. Sometimes they will return to nests they built the year before. Often, they move on, giving homes to other birds that also nest in tree cavities.

Wood ducks are one of many animals that need both forest and water. Others include bald eagles, osprey, and river otters.

Salmon, trout, and trees all need one another. Even old trees that die and fall into the water help fish by giving them hiding places. Big old trees protect tiny fish that grow into giant salmon that return to forest streams to lay their eggs.

Beavers are the carpenters of the tree bottoms. They chop trees for food and for building dams, lodges, and new stream channels. Trees have been found to grow faster when living near a beaver's pond.

Herons help us see how a forest is only part of a larger piece of the land called an ecosystem. Ecosystems are where lots of plants and animals share homes over a large land area. Herons need the forest part of the ecosystem for nesting. They need the water for feeding on fish, frogs, and salamanders.

Lots of hawks need forests. The one you will see more often than any is the red-tail. That is because it lives on the edge of forests or small woodlands. Hawks that live deep within larger forests are the Cooper's hawk, goshawk, and sharp-shinned hawk.

Size is one good way to tell a black bear from a grizzly. The grizzly also has a hunched look to its shoulders. Both kinds can be brown, honey-colored, and even cinnamon, but only the grizzly is in danger of extinction.

Rarest of forest owls, the spotted owls live only in the last ancient forests of the Northwest. These old forests offer safe nesting places where the tallest trees on earth also live, the Douglas firs and redwoods. Just one pair of owls may need as much as 3,000 acres to raise its young.

Great blue heron

Grizzly bear

Spotted owl

Tips to Help You Find Animals in the Forest

Watch the ground for tracks, drawing each new one you find. Learn new tracks by following animals you see or by looking in field guides for tracks and sign.

Listen to the songs of birds. Each sings a song all its own. Record the songs if your parents have the equipment. Or, memorize them like a new spelling word or the lyrics to a song you enjoy.

Follow a stream. Most forest animals need both the water and trees to survive, so this is the best of places. Muddy banks are great for tracks of raccoons and deer or for finding salamanders, toads, and tree frogs.

No two forests are alike, so animals will be found in one and not another. So, have fun visiting as many different forests as you can.

Visit early. Visit late. Mornings are best.

Night may be the only time to hear some owls. But watch for them sleeping by day, tucked close to a tree trunk.

Always walk with a parent or trusted adult, sharing your discoveries and learning from others.

Find a single tree often visited by birds. Watch it all year long, getting to know the ways animals use it from day to day, month to month.

Think of a forest as a house. It is a place with many rooms, including a kitchen which supplies food. Find a small area with lots of seeds, berries, or water and you will likely see animals return. You might also see baby animals in spring.